The Three Gorges

Watercolor Paintings

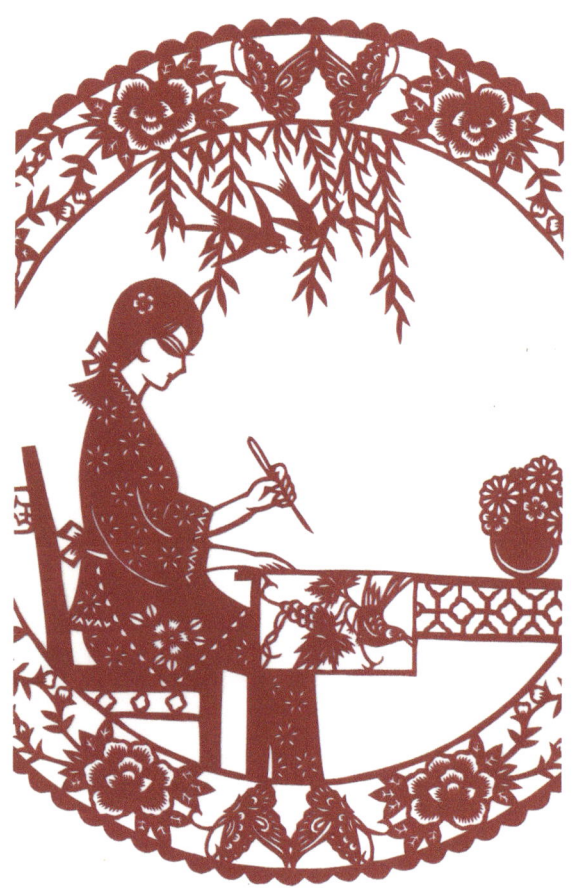

CONTENTS

Preface

Situated in the southwest of China, the Three Gorges on the Yangtze River, including the Whistling-Pool Gorge, the Witch Gorge, and the West-Hill Gorge, are not only famous for their spectacular natural scenery, but also well-known for their historical and cultural significance. However, much of the region, along with many historic spots and archeological sites, is submerged in the water following the completion of China's Three Gorges Dam Project.

The first of the Three Gorges is the Whistling-Pool Gorge, also known as the Peeping-Gate Gorge. Located right downstream of the ancient village of White-King, passing between the Flaming-Red-Armor Mountain on the north and the White-Cliff Mountain on the south at the entrance, it was once the most spectacular, but shortest and narrowest gorge, only 5 miles long and 300-500 feet wide. The mountains on both riversides once soared aloft to as high as 4,000 feet, creating spectacular vistas.

The second of the Three Gorges is the Witch Gorge. Stretching for 28 miles through the Witch Mountains on both riversides, it was once considered as the most serene, secluded, and beautiful gorge. Among the twelve magnificent peaks of the Witch Mountains, the Goddess Peak is the most charming one. Legend has it that it is the incarnation of a fairy that helped the boats navigate through the river as well as the Great Yu control the flood in ancient times.

The third of the Three Gorges is the West-Hill Gorge. Extending eastward through the magnificent mountains for nearly half of the entire distance as far as the West-Hill Mountain, it was once the longest, but most treacherous gorge. Actually it was a series of four separate gorges, including the Gorge of Tactics Book and Precious Sword, the Gorge of Bull Liver and Horse Lung, the Gorge of Yellow Buffalo, and the Gorge of Shadow Play.

This book showcases a masterpiece collection of original watercolor paintings of the Three Gorges on the Yangtze River before China's Three Gorges Dam Project. It highlights the magnificence and beauty of China's Three Gorges submerged in the mighty torrent of history with unrivaled artistry never before seen. It is a must have historical and cultural art treasure.

The Three Gorges

White Lee

Leaving White-King at colorful sunrise

On a long journey home,

Go for a day's sail through the gorges

Down the river a thousand miles long to sightsee,

Endless cries of apes on both shores

Keep floating across the gorges,

As the sailboat glides

Swiftly past myriads of mountains.

Sail through the Peeping Gate

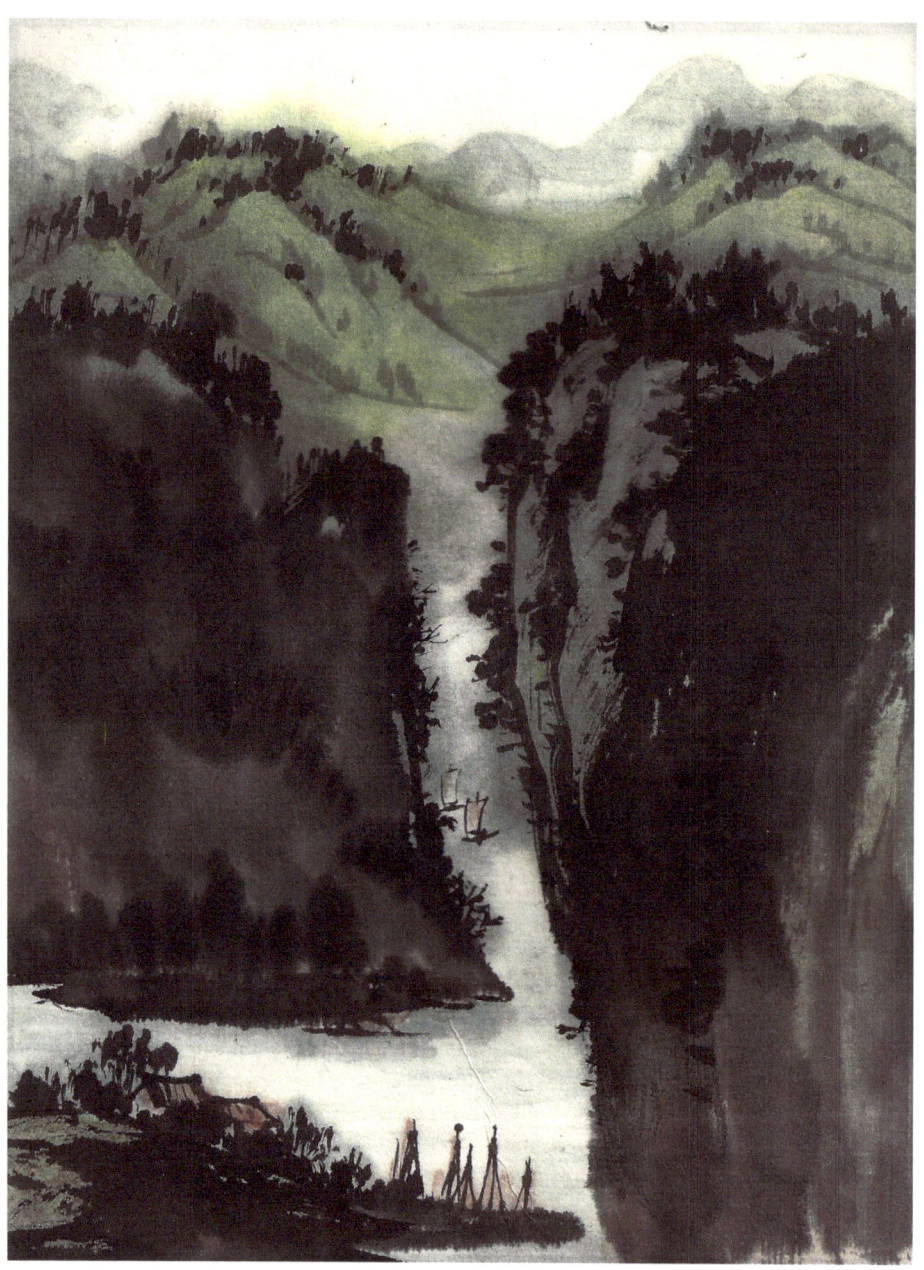

Sail down the Whistling-Pool

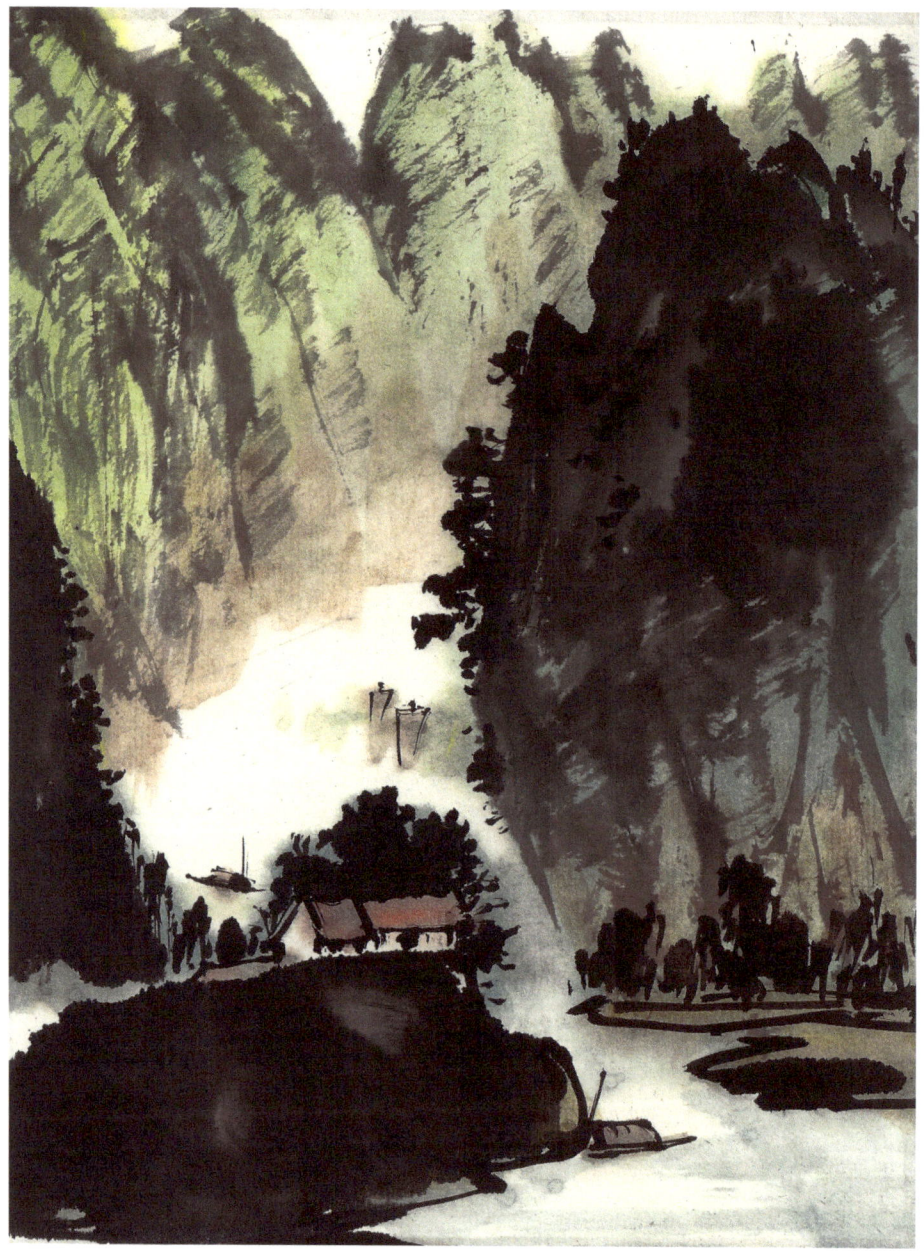

The River-Gazing Pagoda

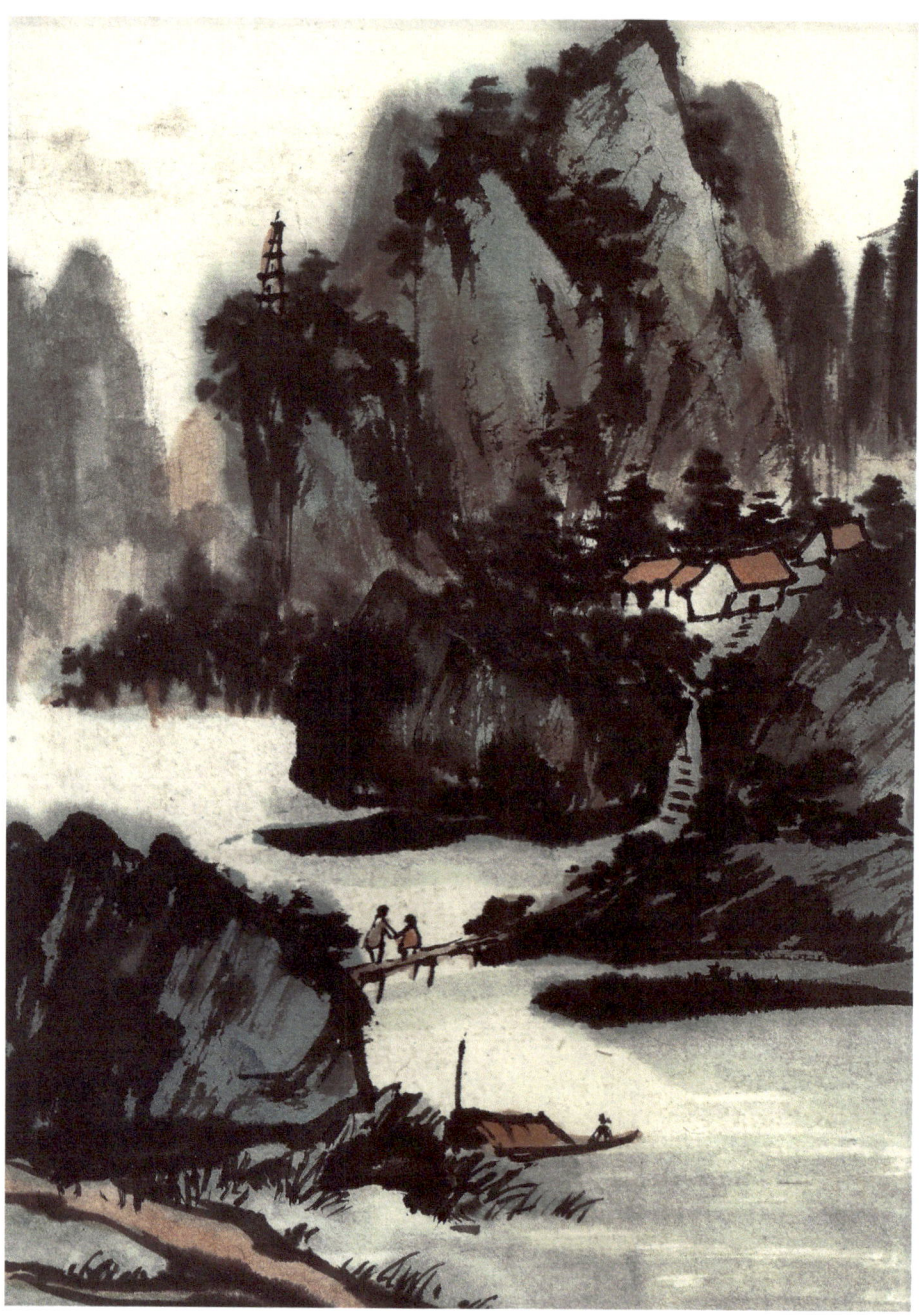

The Heavenly Terrace

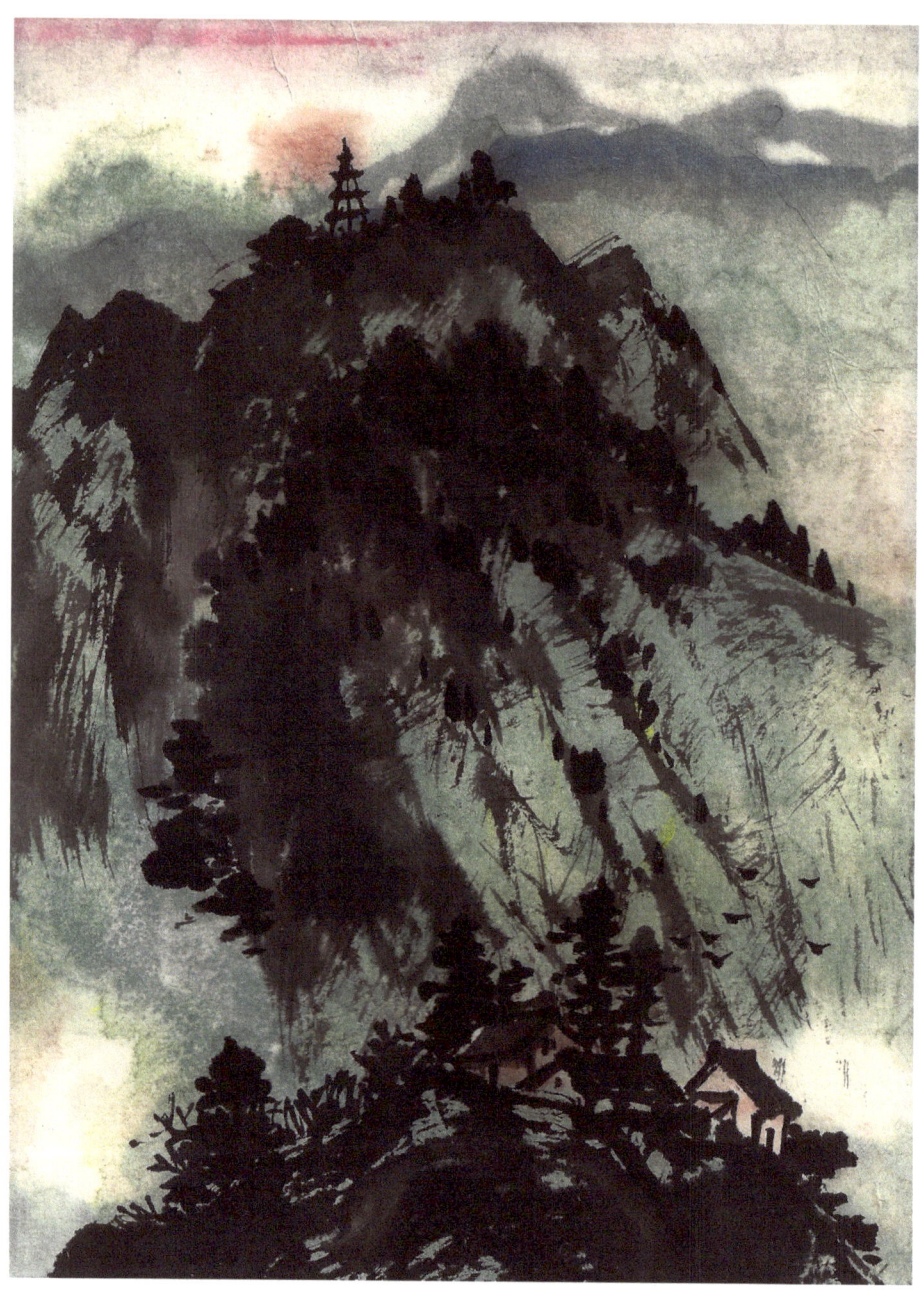

The Waterfall by Cliff Hanger

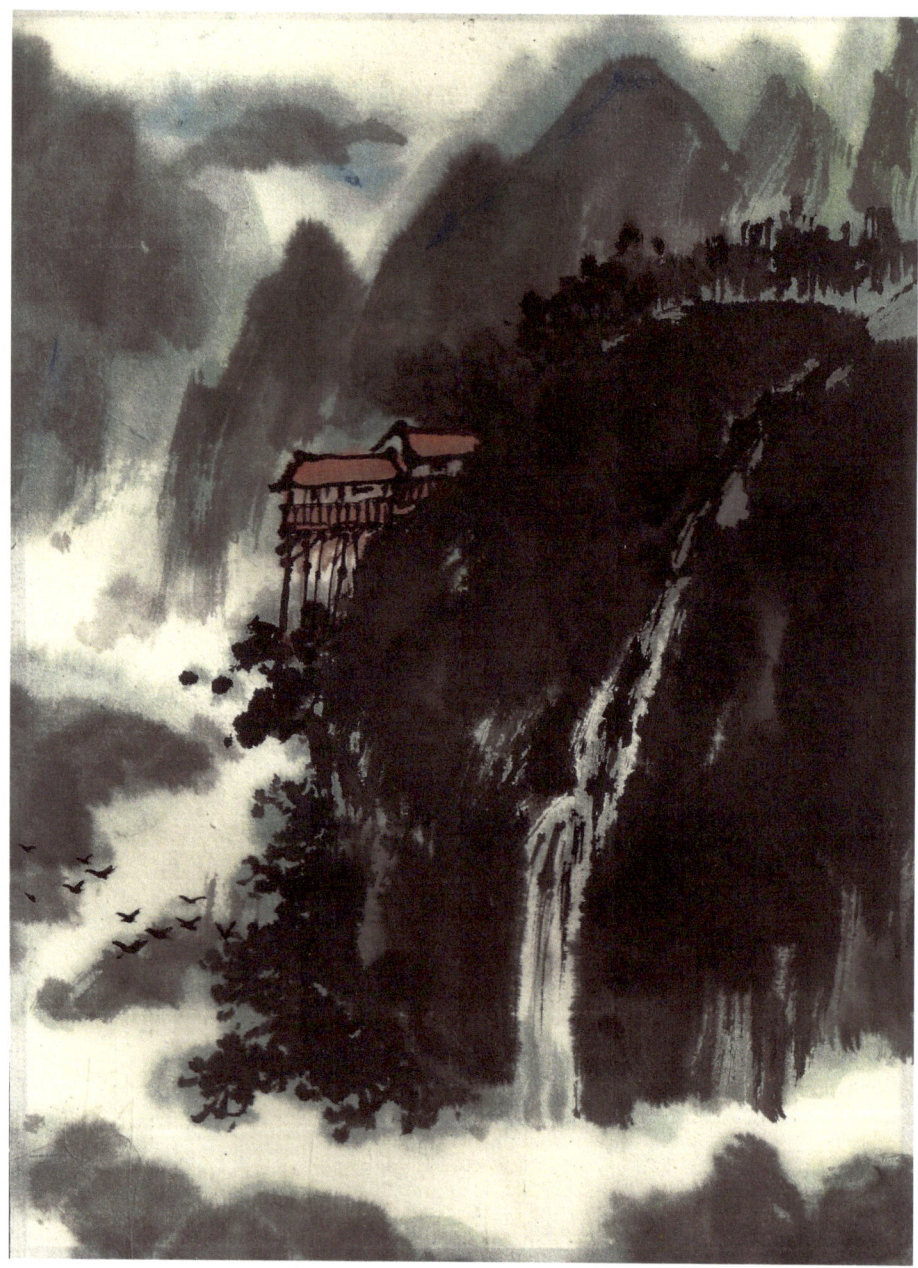

Sail through the Witch Mountains

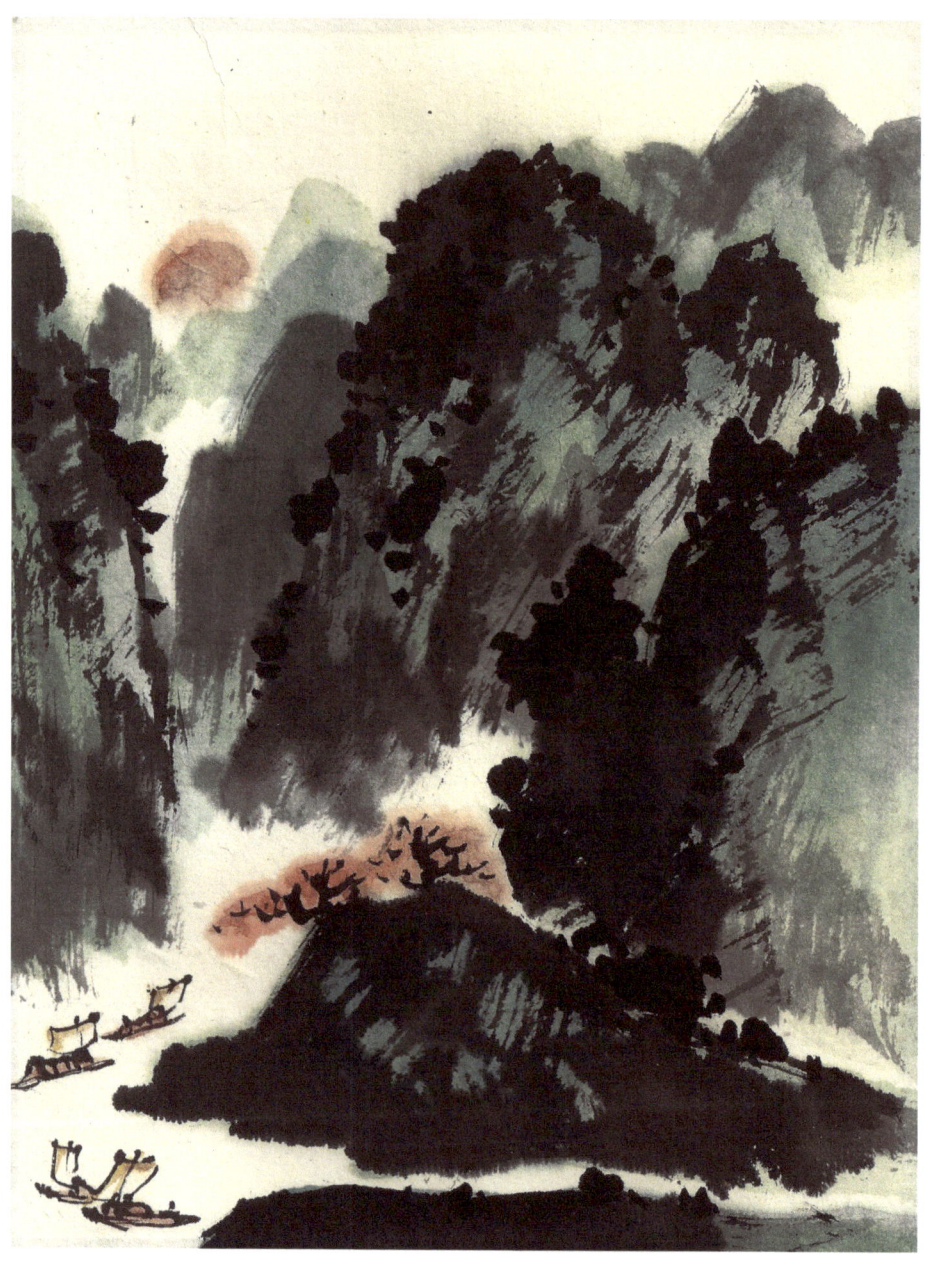

The Goddess Peak

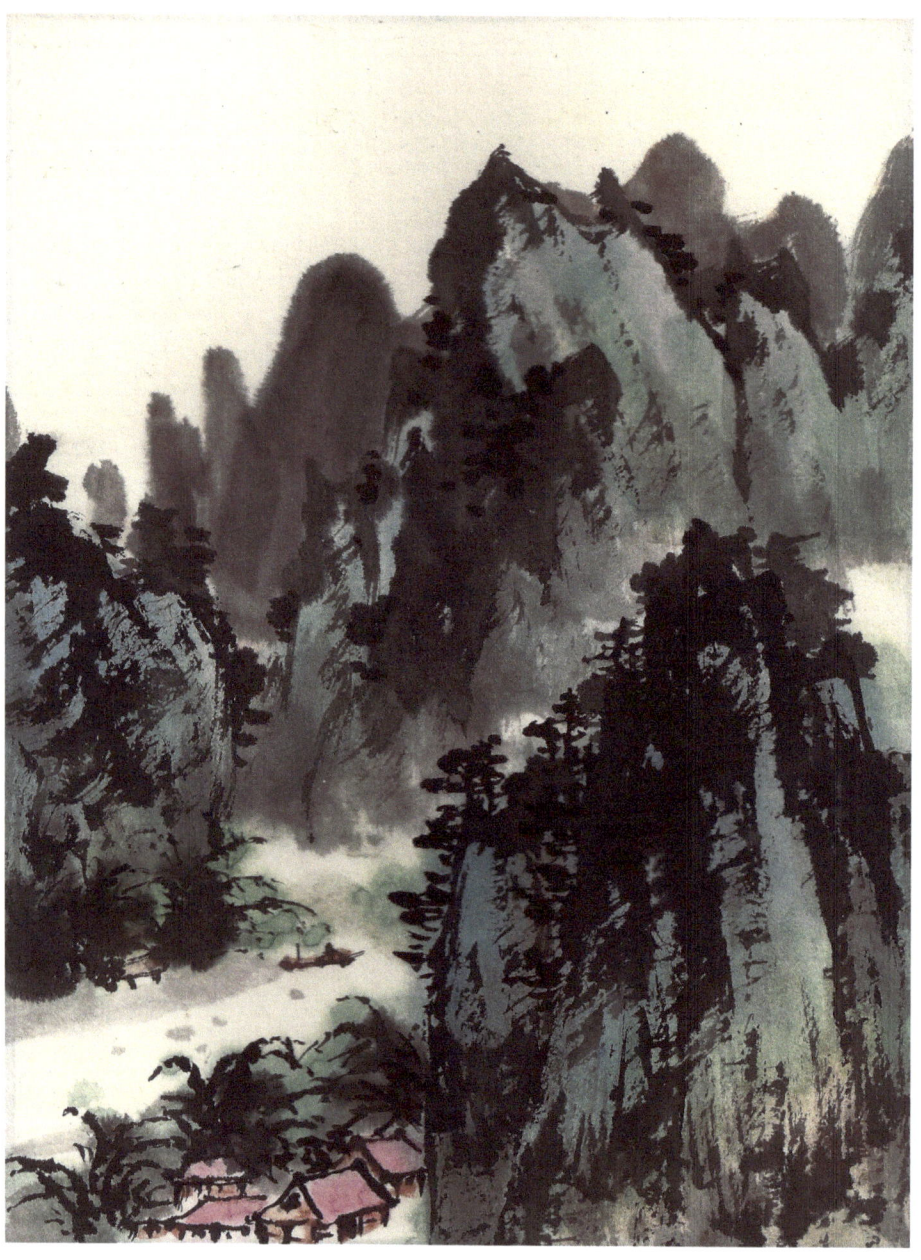

The Fountain Pavilion

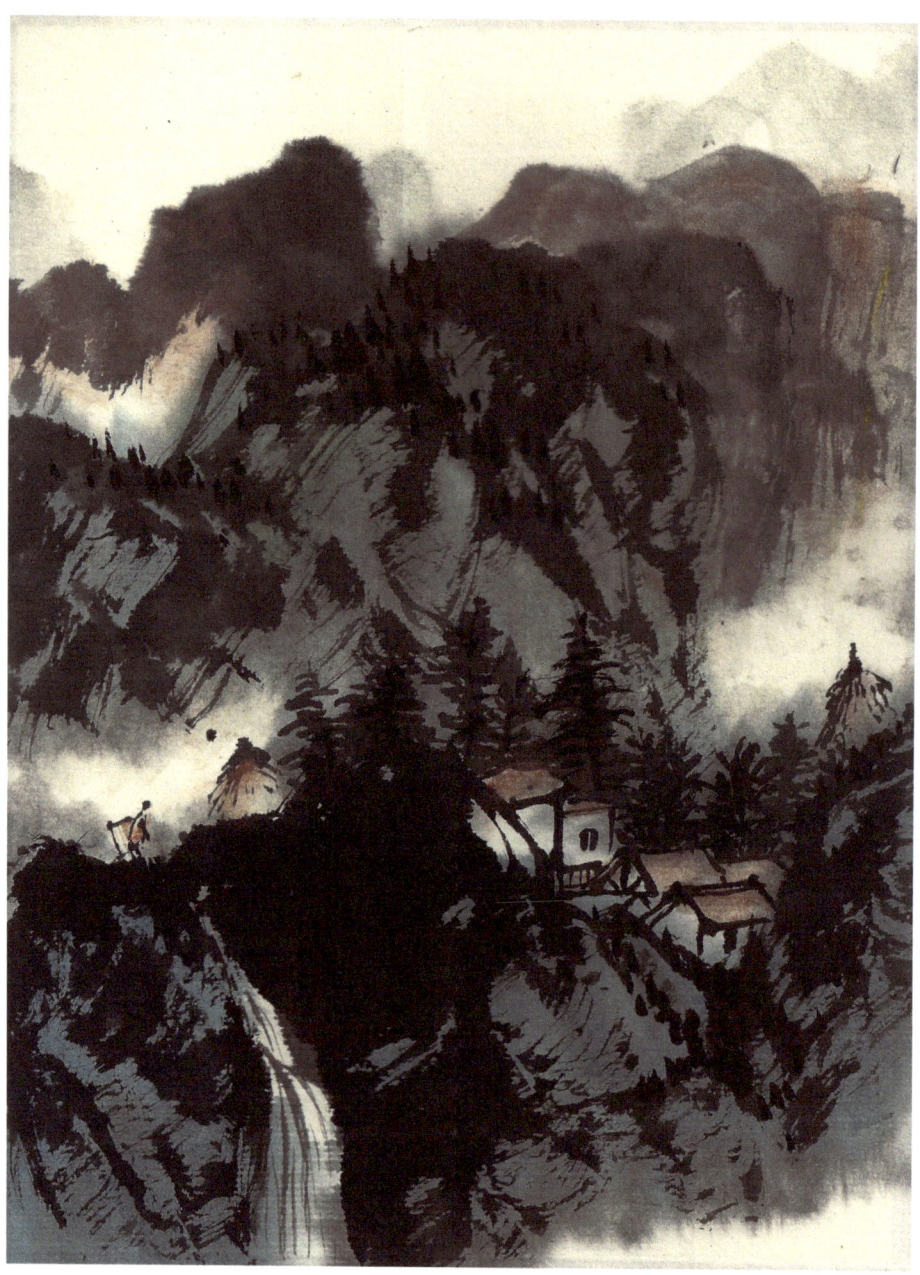

The Immortal Bridge

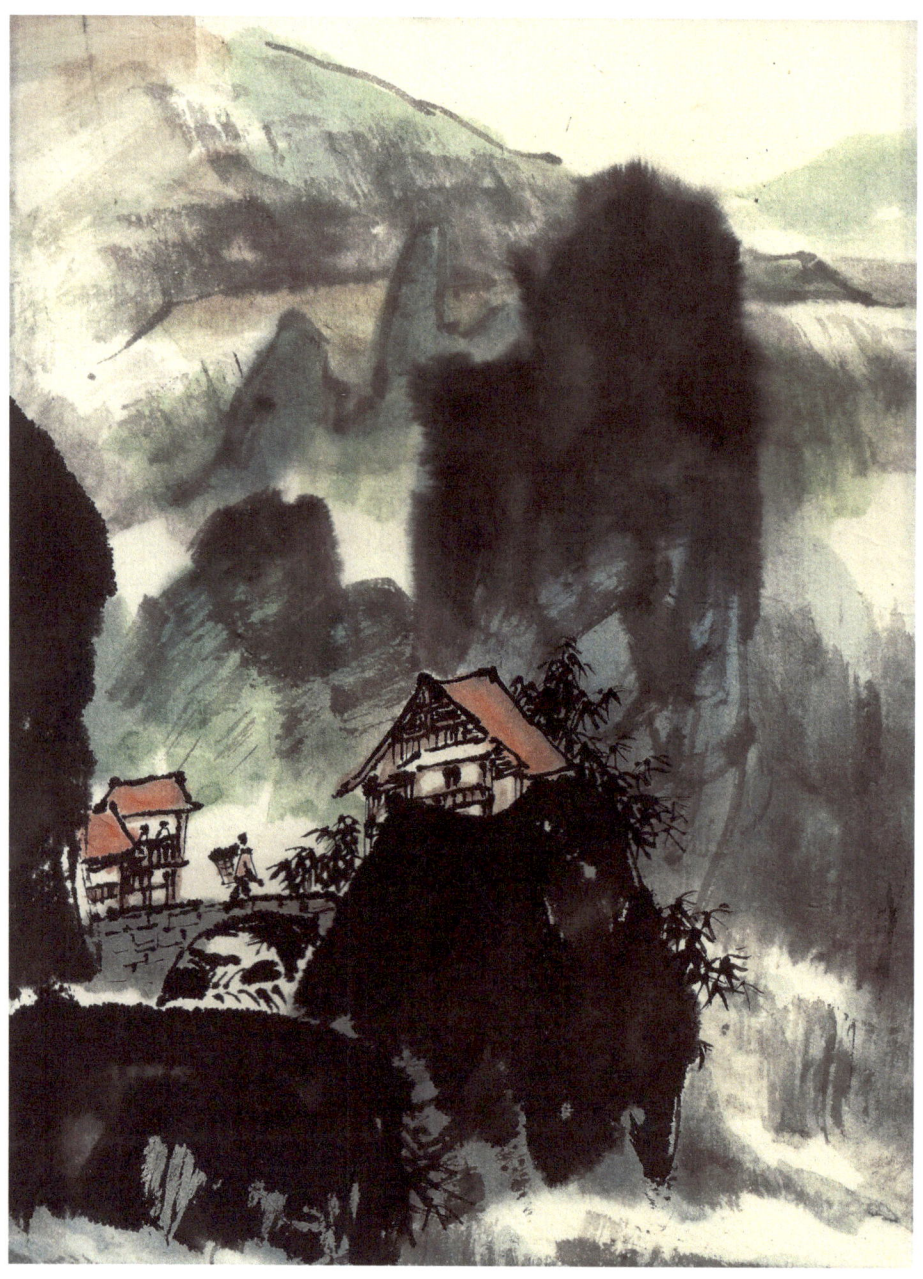

The Twin Dragons' Peak

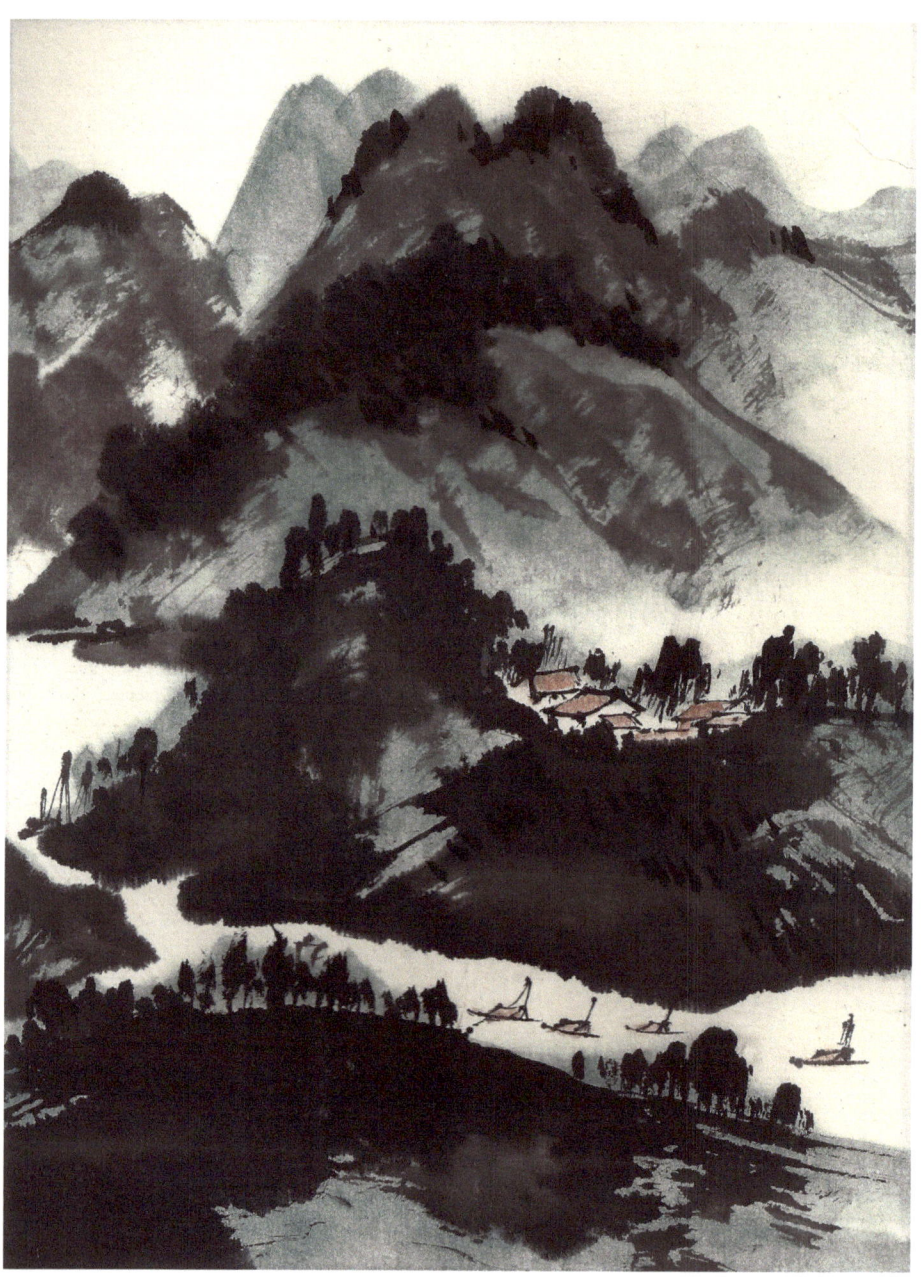

Heavenly Gate of Sunrays

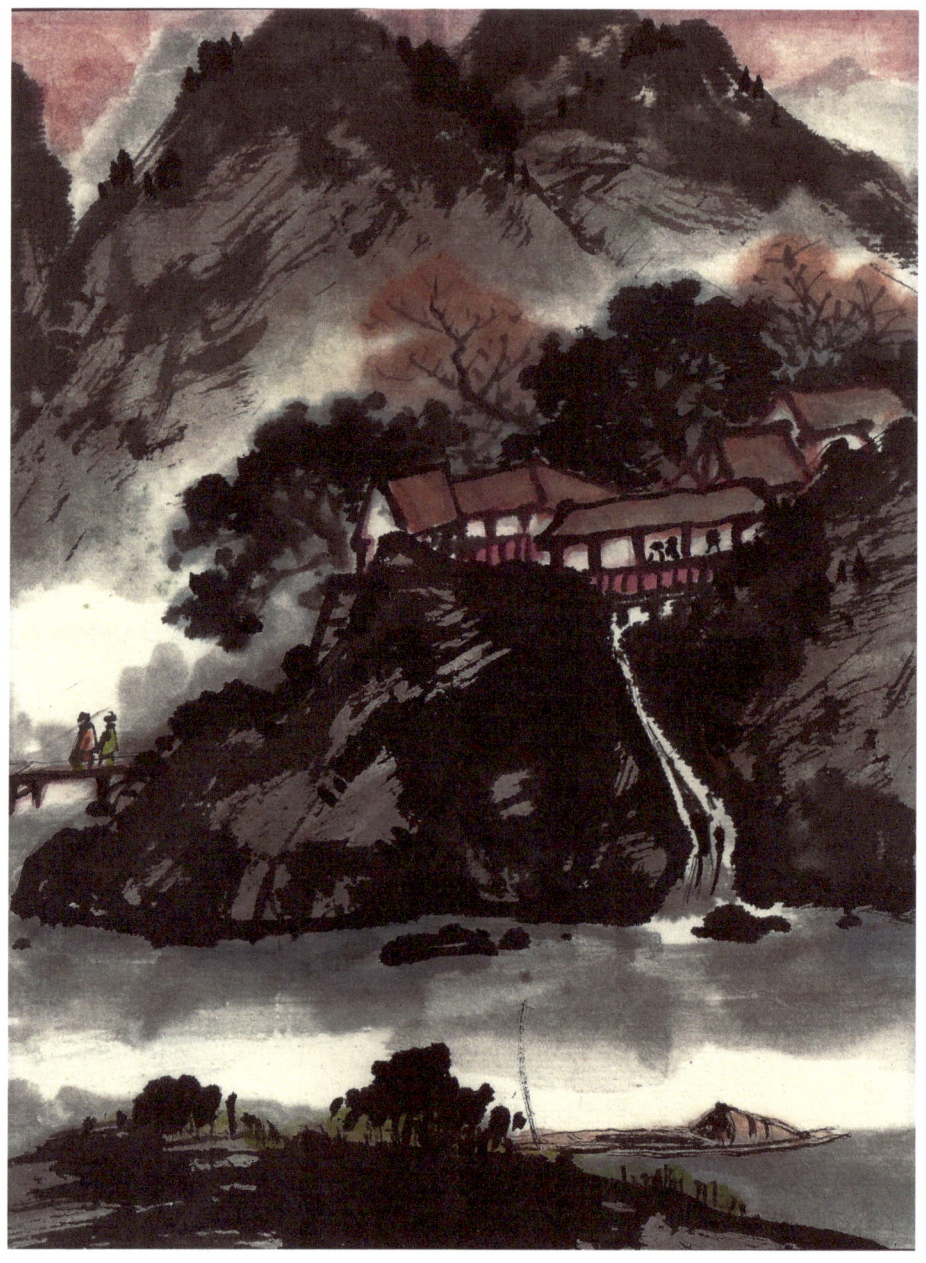

The City of Ghosts

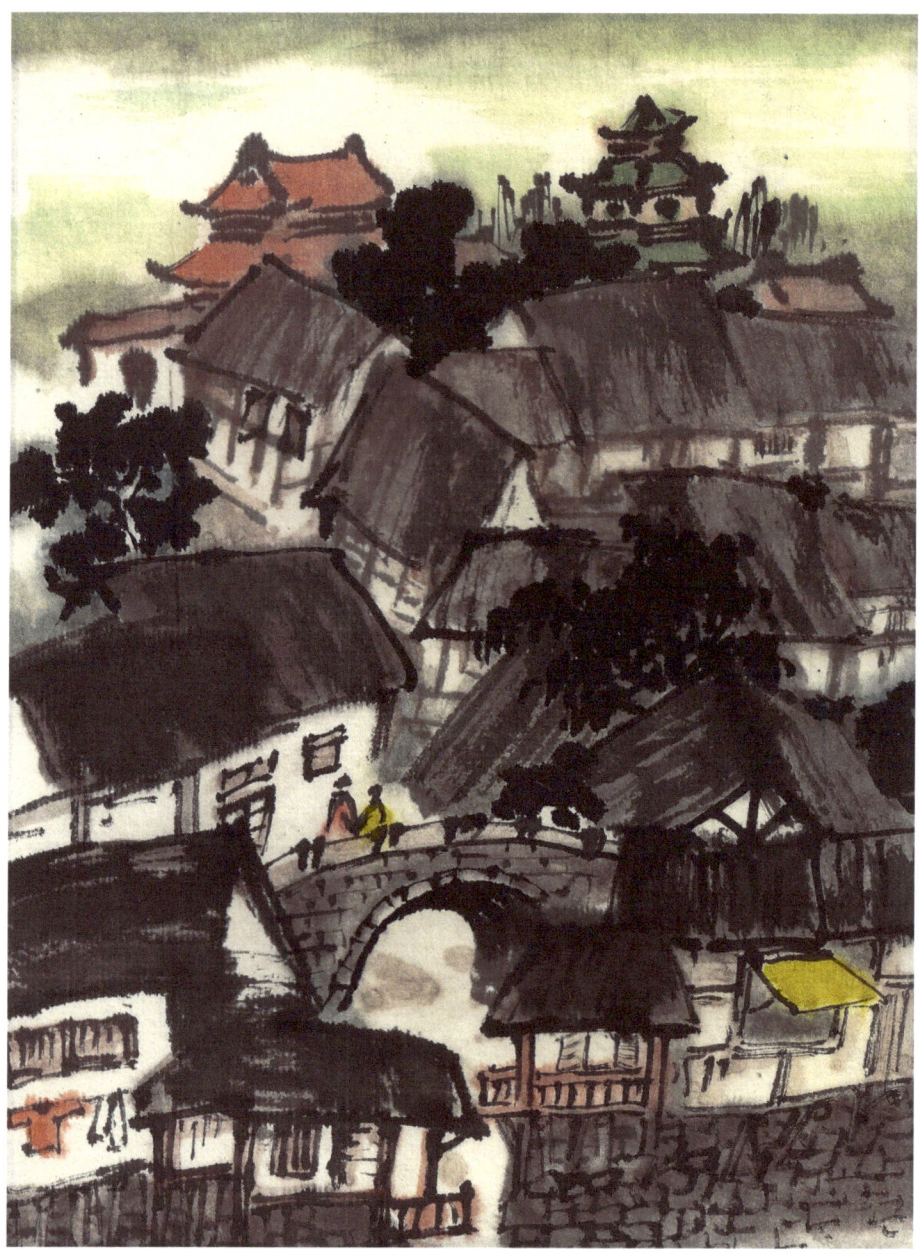

Autumn Riverside

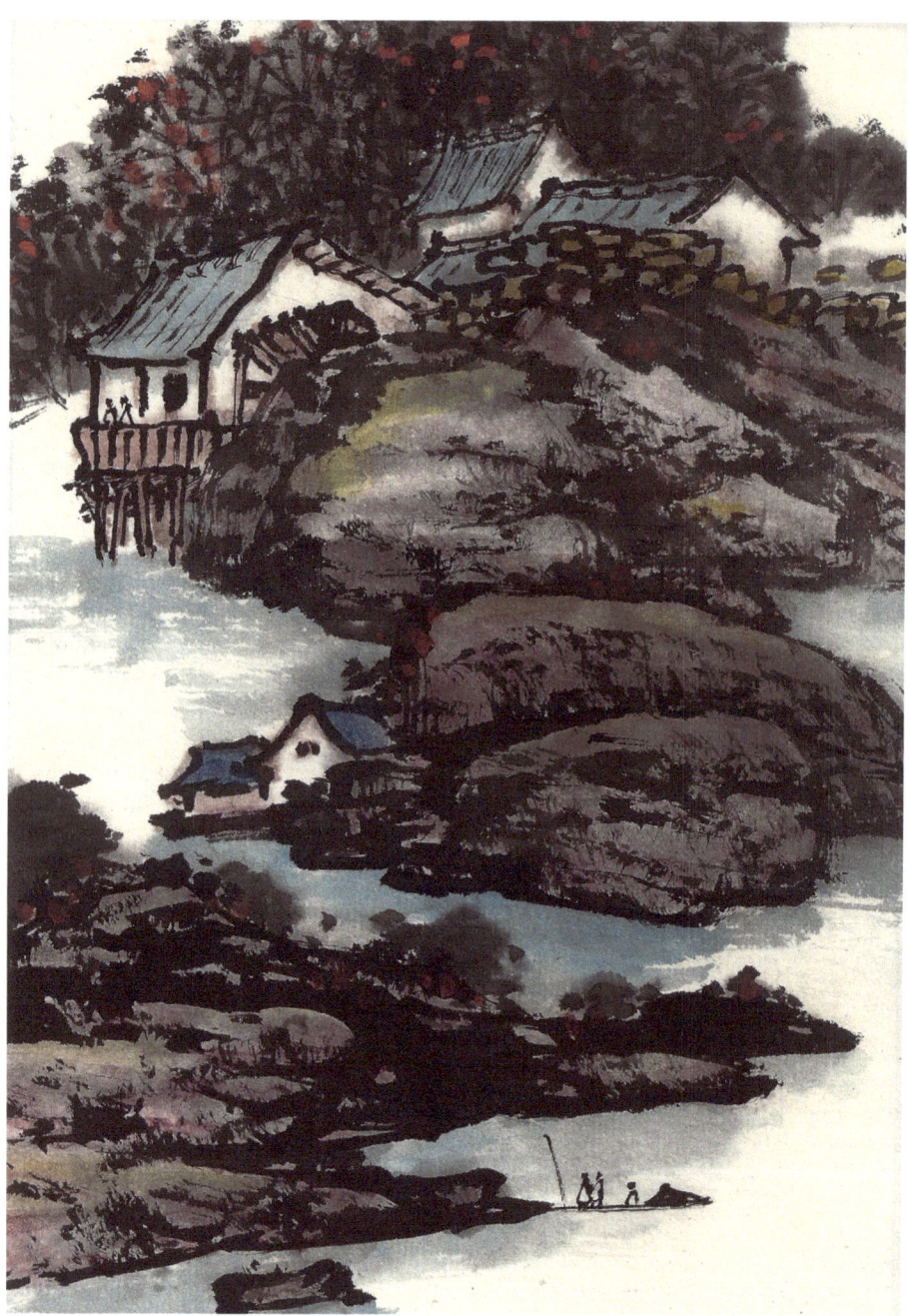

The Great Passage

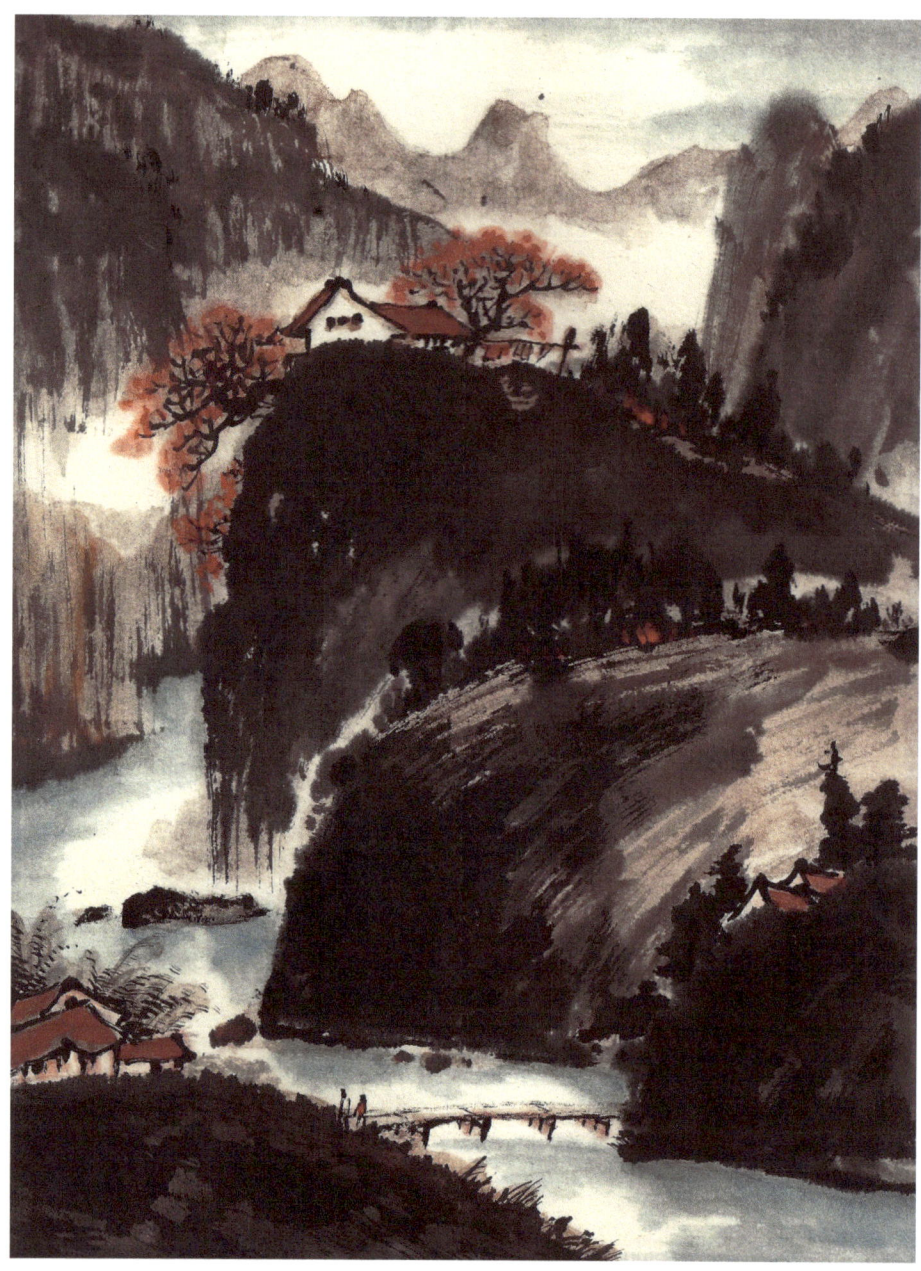

The Resolute Rock

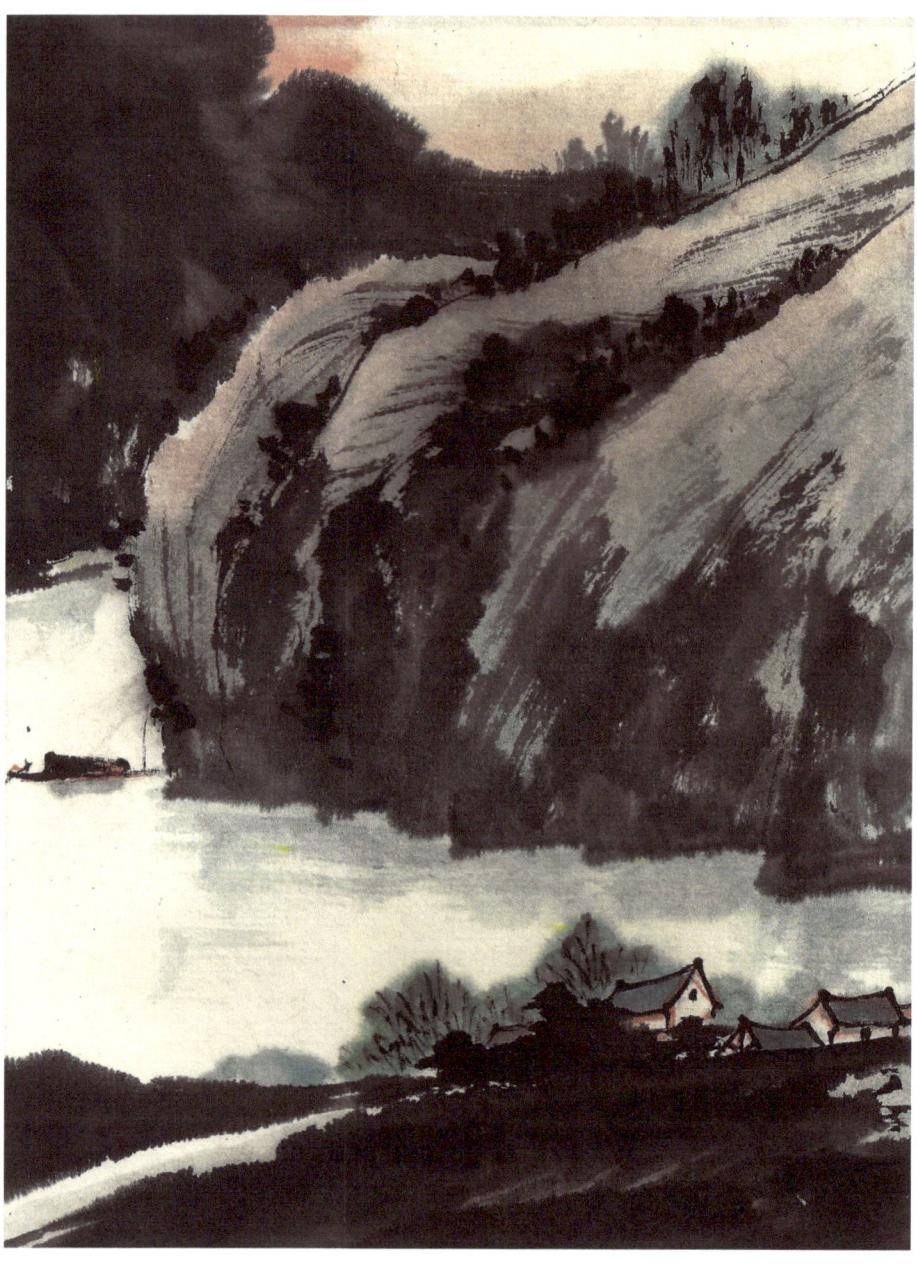

Sails by the Plum Sandalwood Grove

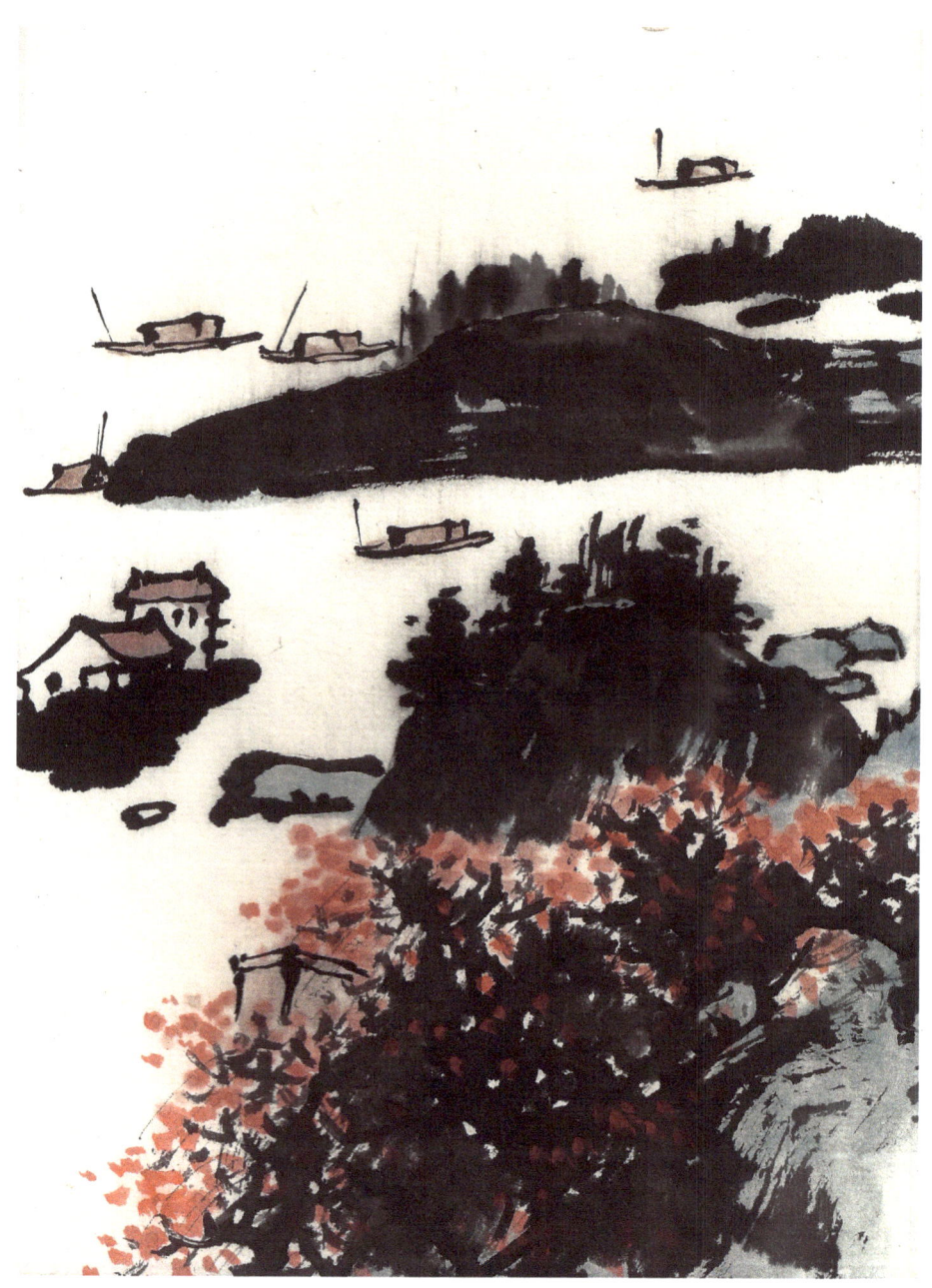

The Cloud-Capped Pavilion

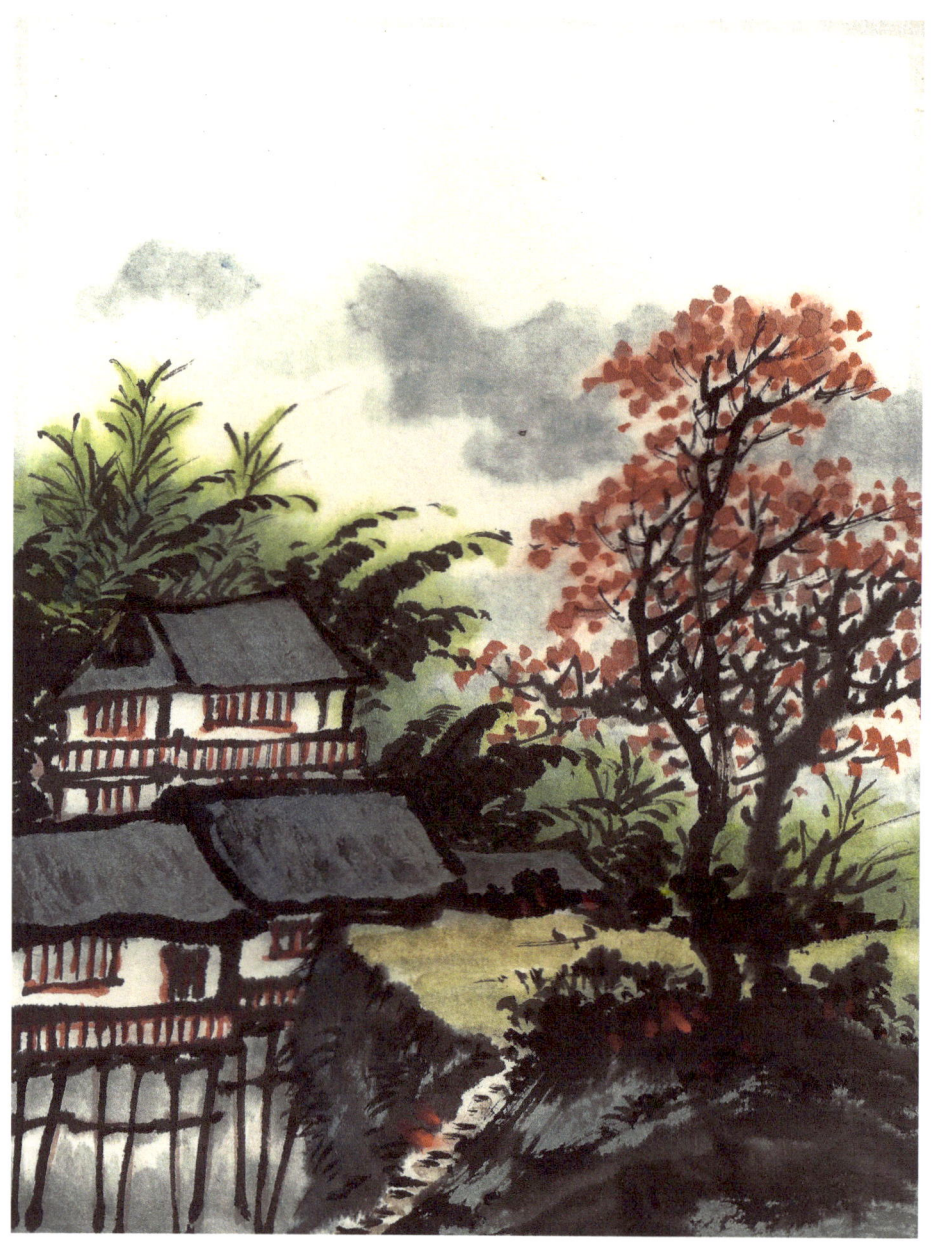

Shadow Play

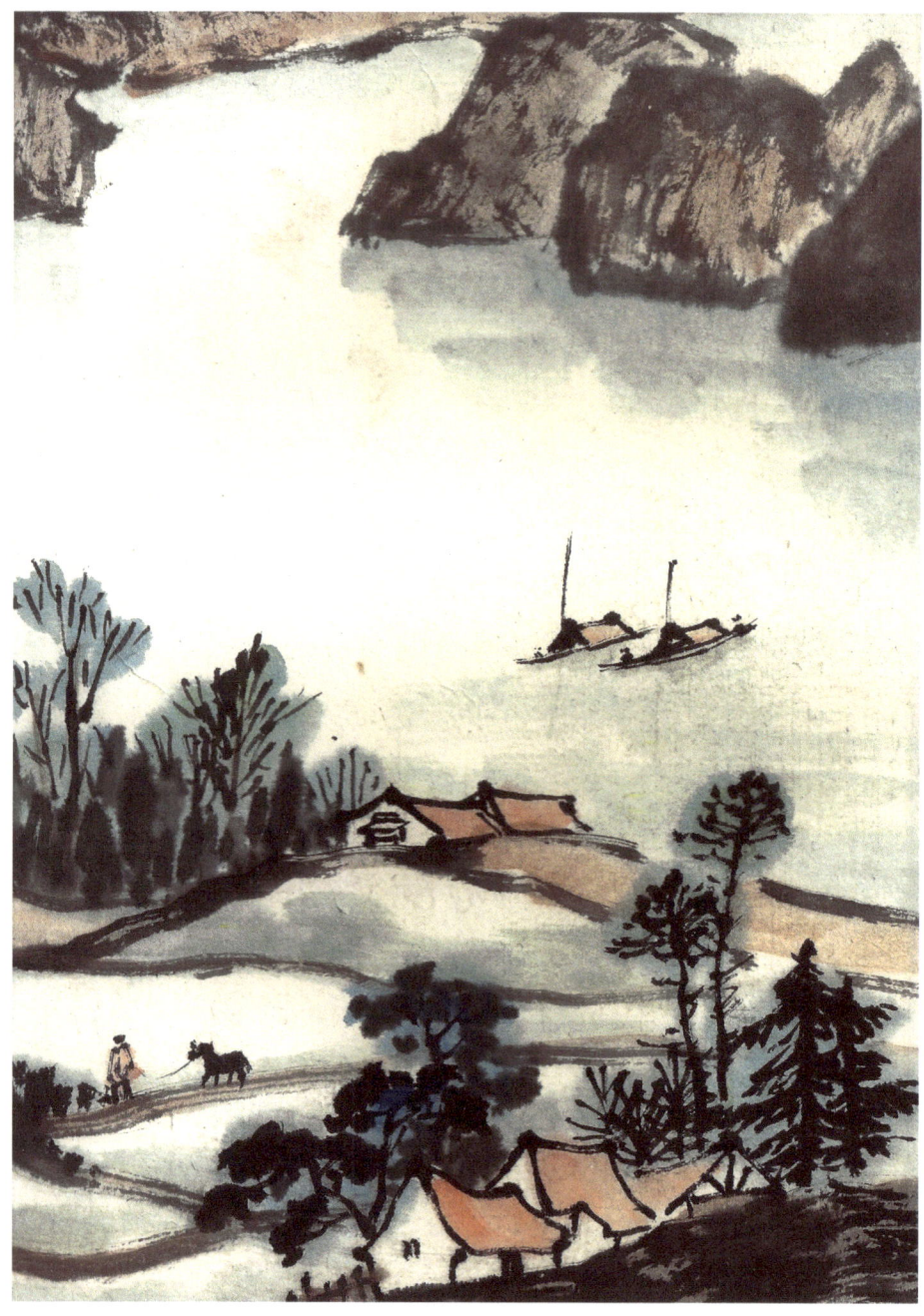

The Sunset on Sunny Hill

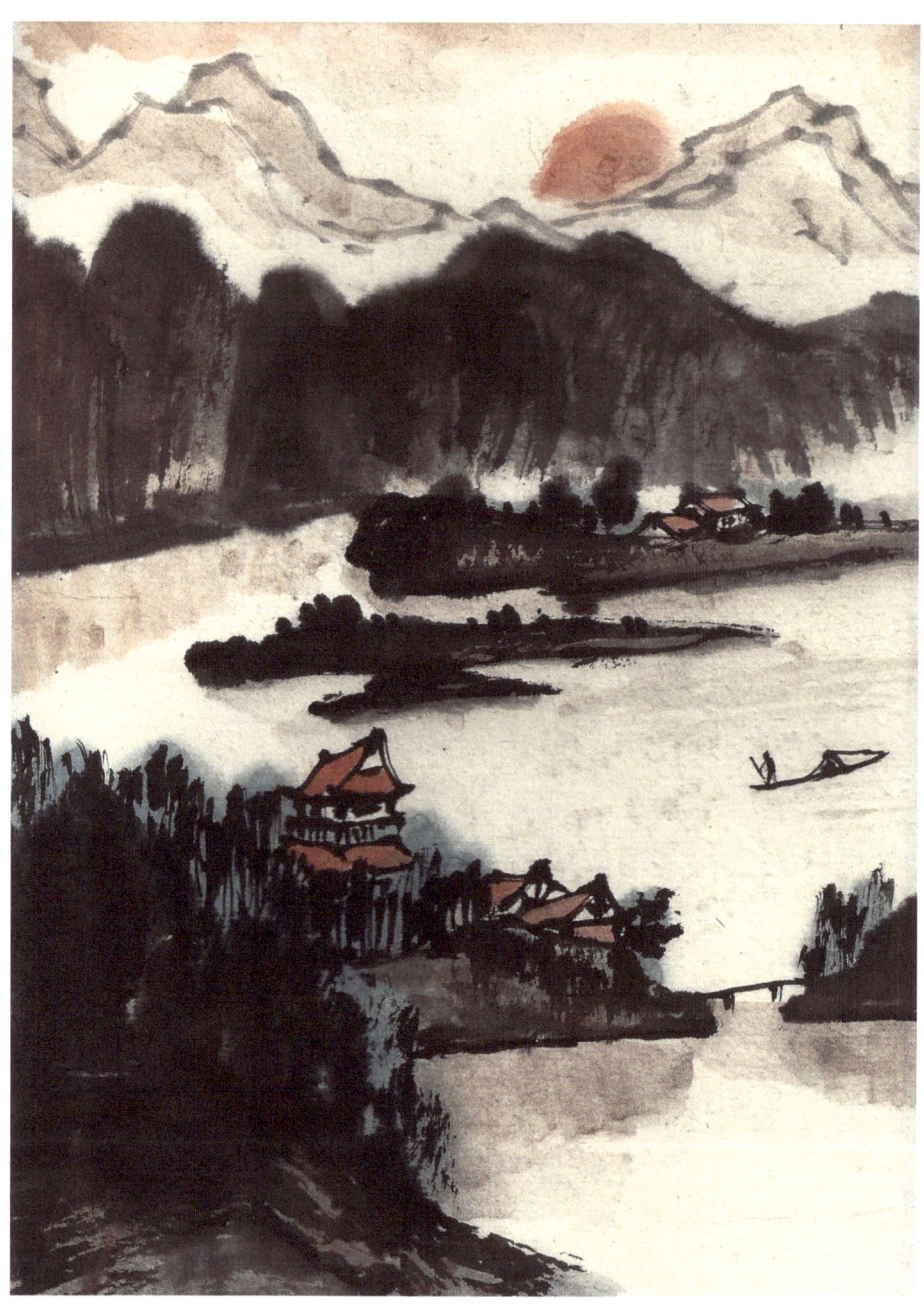

Lifelines on the Yangtze River

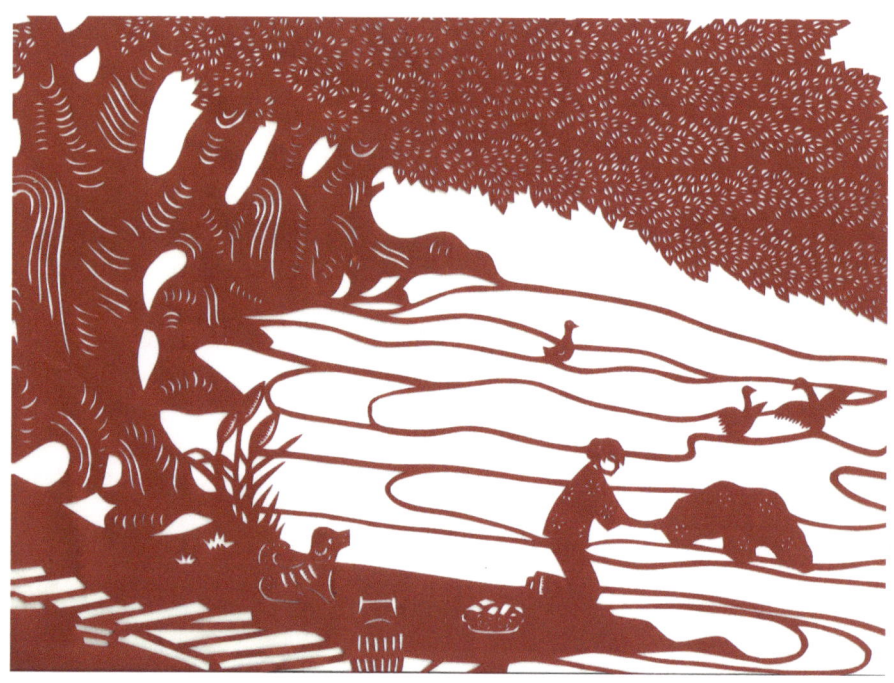

www.ingramcontent.com/pod-product-compliance
Lightning Source LLC
Chambersburg PA
CBHW041206180526
45172CB00006B/1211